DEAR GOD, I'M ANXIOUS

90 Days of Faith, Peace, and
Scripture for Teen Girls Struggling
with Anxiety and Overwhelm

DOROTHY ASTER

YOU ARE NOT ALONE

"So do not fear, for I am with you; do not be dismayed, for I am your God. I will strengthen you and help you; I will uphold you with my righteous right hand."

Isaiah 41:10

DEVOTION

In uncertain times, remembering that we are surrounded by love and companionship can lift us beyond our worries.

REFLECTION

What are some situations in your life where you feel most alone, and how might you invite God into those moments?

_____

_____

_____

_____

PRAYER

Dear God, thank you for always being by my side, even when I feel alone. Please remind me of your presence in my everyday life and help me to lean on you when anxiety starts to creep in.

Remember, you are never truly alone; God is with you every step of the way.

GOD'S PROMISES IN UNCERTAIN TIMES

"Trust in the Lord with all your heart, and lean not on your own understanding; in all your ways acknowledge Him, and He will make your paths straight."

Proverbs 3:5-6

DEVOTION

In moments of uncertainty, remember that embracing God's guidance often leads to clarity and peace that we cannot find on our own.

REFLECTION

What worries are currently weighing on your heart, and how can you remind yourself of God's promises during this uncertain time?

_____

_____

_____

_____

PRAYER

Dear God, I lift up my worries and uncertainties to You. Please help me to find peace in Your promises and trust that You are with me always. Amen.

Even in chaos, His promises remain our anchor.

FINDING CALM IN THE STORM

"Cast all your anxiety on him because he cares for you."

1 Peter 5:7

DEVOTION

In moments of chaos, surrendering our worries to a caring presence can bring unexpected peace and clarity.

REFLECTION

What storms are you facing in your life right now, and how can you invite calm into those moments of anxiety?

_____

_____

_____

_____

PRAYER

Dear God, I ask for your peace to wash over this young heart in times of fear and uncertainty. Help her to feel your presence and to trust that she is never alone in the storm.

Even in the fiercest storms, calm can be found in the gentle whisper of God's love.

LETTING GO OF PERFECTIONISM

"Whatever you do, work heartily, as for the Lord and not for men, knowing that from the Lord you will receive the inheritance as your reward."

Colossians 3:23-24

DEVOTION

Remember, it's in our imperfections that our true selves shine through, and embracing our humanity is a beautiful part of growth.

REFLECTION

What would your life look like if you embraced your unique journey instead of striving for an impossible standard? Imagine the freedom you would feel if you let go of the need to be perfect and gave yourself permission to be beautifully yourself.

_____

_____

_____

_____

PRAYER

Dear God, help me to release the hold perfectionism has over my heart. Teach me to find joy in my journey and to appreciate my authentic self, flaws and all. Amen.

Perfection is not the goal; growth and grace are.

PRAYING THROUGH PANIC

"Do not be anxious about anything, but in every situation, by prayer and petition, with thanksgiving, present your requests to God. And the peace of God, which transcends all understanding, will guard your hearts and your minds in Christ Jesus."

Philippians 4:6–7

DEVOTION

Even amidst the chaos of anxiety, bringing your worries to God can transform fear into peace, reminding us that we are never alone.

REFLECTION

What does panic feel like for you, and how have you seen prayer help in those moments of distress? When you think about bringing your worries to God, what words come to mind?

_____

_____

_____

_____

PRAYER

Dear God, thank you for being a listening ear in my moments of panic. Help me to feel Your presence with me and guide my thoughts when anxiety tries to take over.

Even in the chaos, prayer is an anchor that steadies the soul.

THE POWER OF GRATITUDE

"Give thanks to the Lord, for He is good; His love endures forever."

Psalm 107:1

DEVOTION

Gratitude has the unique ability to illuminate the beautiful moments in our lives, reminding us that even amidst chaos, there is always something to cherish.

REFLECTION

What are three things you can be grateful for today, even in the midst of your worries? Think about small moments or people that bring you joy.

_____

_____

_____

_____

PRAYER

Dear God, thank You for the little blessings that surround us each day. Help me to see the light in the darkness and to carry a heart full of gratitude.

Gratitude turns what we have into enough.

RESTING IN GOD'S LOVE

"How precious is your steadfast love, O God! The children of mankind take refuge in the shadow of your wings."

Psalm 36:7

DEVOTION

Trusting in God's unwavering love helps us blossom even in the most trying times.

REFLECTION

What does it mean to you to truly rest in God's love during your most anxious moments? Can you think of a time when you felt His peace amid your worries?

_____

_____

_____

_____

PRAYER

Dear God, thank You for always being a source of love and comfort in our lives. Help me to remember that I can find rest in You, especially when I feel overwhelmed. Amen.

Rest isn't just about stopping; it's about trusting that God holds your worries close.

OVERCOMING SOCIAL ANXIETY

"Cast all your anxiety on him because he cares for you"

1 Peter 5:7

DEVOTION

Embracing small, brave steps can help us conquer the fears that bind us.

REFLECTION

What thoughts come to your mind when you're in social situations that make you feel anxious? How might you see yourself differently if you embraced your uniqueness instead of comparing yourself to others?

_____

_____

_____

_____

PRAYER

Dear God, thank You for being with me in every situation. Help me to feel Your presence when I'm anxious, guiding me to embrace who I am and find peace in Your love.

You are more than your fears; you are beautifully made with courage within.

SURRENDERING WORRY ABOUT THE FUTURE

"For I know the plans I have for you,"
says the Lord, "

Jeremiah 29:11

DEVOTION

Trusting in God's plan allows us to
move forward without being overtaken
by the anxiety of the unknown.

REFLECTION

What are the specific worries you have about your future, and how do they make you feel in your daily life?

_____

_____

_____

_____

PRAYER

Dear God, help me release my worries and trust in Your plans for my future. Remind me that I am never alone and that You hold everything in Your hands. Fill me with peace as I choose to rely on You.

Letting go of worry is the first step towards embracing hope.

SAFE IN
GOD'S PRESENCE

"God is our refuge and strength, an ever-present help in trouble. Therefore we will not fear, though the earth give way and the mountains fall into the heart of the sea, though its waters roar and foam and the mountains quake with their surging."

Psalm 46:1-3

DEVOTION

In God's presence, there is a refuge that calms our anxious hearts, allowing us to trust in His unwavering love and support.

REFLECTION

What does it feel like for you to know that you are safe in God's presence, especially when you're feeling anxious or overwhelmed? How can you remind yourself of that safety in your daily life?

_____

_____

_____

_____

PRAYER

Dear God, thank You for being a safe haven in my life. Help me to feel Your comforting presence, especially in moments of anxiety, and remind me that I am never alone.

In the shelter of His presence, our fears can find rest.

QUIETING THE INNER CRITIC

"Focus on what is true, noble, right, pure, lovely, admirable—things that are excellent and praiseworthy."

Philippians 4:8

DEVOTION

Sometimes, the loudest voice we hear is our own, and learning to replace criticism with compassion opens the door to self-acceptance and growth.

REFLECTION

What negative words or phrases does your inner critic use against you, and how might you counter them with kindness and truth?

_____

_____

_____

_____

PRAYER

Dear God, help me to quiet the harsh voice of my inner critic and replace it with Your gentle truth. Fill my heart with Your love and remind me that I am enough, just as I am.

Your worth is not defined by perfection, but by the love that exists within you.

COURAGE TO
BE YOURSELF

Isaiah 43:1-4 reminds us that we are precious in God's sight and that He has called us by name. When we understand our inherent worth, we can find the courage to embrace our true selves.

DEVOTION

Embracing your true self is the gateway to authentic relationships and unshakeable confidence.

REFLECTION

What does it mean to you to have the courage to be yourself, especially when you feel pressure to fit in with others?

_____

_____

_____

_____

PRAYER

Dear God, help me to embrace who I am and give me the strength to share my true self with the world. Guide me through moments of doubt, reminding me that I am beautifully created and loved just as I am.

Courage is not the absence of fear, but the decision to embrace your unique, beautiful self despite it.

TRUSTING WHEN YOU CAN'T SEE

"Be still and know that I am God."

Psalm 46:10

DEVOTION

Even when life feels uncertain and we can't see what lies ahead, trust that God is crafting something beautiful from our struggles.

REFLECTION

What are some things in your life right now that feel uncertain or unclear, and how might trusting in something bigger than yourself help you cope with that uncertainty?

_____

_____

_____

_____

PRAYER

Dear God, help me to embrace the uncertainty of this moment and find peace in trusting You. Give me the strength to let go of my worries and hold onto Your promises. Amen.

Trust is the light that guides us through the darkness of uncertainty.

LEARNING TO SAY NO

"If you find honey, eat just enough—too much of it, and you will vomit."

Proverbs 25:16

DEVOTION

Understanding your own limits is essential; it's okay to protect your peace by saying no to what doesn't align with your values.

REFLECTION

What situations make you feel pressured to say yes, even when you truly want to say no? How might setting boundaries in those moments bring you peace?

_____

_____

_____

_____

PRAYER

Dear God, help me find the courage to stand firm in my decisions and to trust that it's okay to prioritize my own needs. Guide me to understand that saying no can be a form of self-care and strength.

Saying no can be an invitation to honor your own heart and well-being.

FRIENDSHIP AND HEALTHY BOUNDARIES

"As iron sharpens iron, so one person sharpens another."

Proverbs 27:17

DEVOTION

Healthy boundaries allow us to nurture our relationships without sacrificing our own well-being.

REFLECTION

What does friendship mean to you, and how do you think healthy boundaries play a role in making those friendships stronger and more fulfilling?

_____

_____

_____

_____

PRAYER

Dear God, help me to understand the beauty of friendship and the importance of setting boundaries. Guide me to find joy in my relationships while also honoring my own needs and the needs of my friends.

True friendship thrives on respect, and respect begins with healthy boundaries.

COPİNG WİTH ACADEMİC PRESSURE

"Come to me, all you who are weary and burdened, and I will give you rest. Take my yoke upon you and learn from me, for I am gentle and humble in heart, and you will find rest for your souls. For my yoke is easy and my burden is light."

Matthew 11:28–30

DEVOTION

We can find solace in knowing that we all face pressures, and it's perfectly human to seek help and take time for ourselves.

REFLECTION

What do you feel when you think about your upcoming exams or assignments? Can you identify where that pressure comes from, and what would make it a little easier for you to cope?

_____

_____

_____

_____

PRAYER

Dear God, remind her that she is more than her grades. Grant her peace and clarity as she navigates her studies and help her to seek joy in learning, not just in results.

Your worth is not determined by a number; it shines through in your effort and heart.

HEALING FROM REJECTION

"The Lord is close to the brokenhearted and saves those who are crushed in spirit."

Psalm 34:18

DEVOTION

Sometimes rejection is not a reflection of our worth but a redirection towards the authentic connections we truly need in our lives.

REFLECTION

What feelings surface when you think about times you've felt rejected? How can you embrace those feelings and still find hope in healing?

_____

_____

_____

_____

PRAYER

Dear God, help me to embrace my feelings of rejection and guide me in finding strength and healing through Your love. Let me remember that I am not alone in this journey and that You are always with me.

Healing begins when we recognize our worth beyond the opinions of others.

DEALING WITH CHANGE

"Forget the former things; do not dwell on the past. See, I am doing a new thing! Now it springs up; do you not perceive it? I am making a way in the wilderness and streams in the wasteland."

Isaiah 43:18–19

DEVOTION

Embrace change as an opportunity for growth, and remember that connection with others can ease the burden of uncertainty.

REFLECTION

What changes are happening in your life right now that feel overwhelming? How might you see these changes as opportunities for growth instead of obstacles?

_____

_____

_____

_____

PRAYER

Dear God, please grant me the peace to accept the changes in my life and the strength to embrace new beginnings. Help me to trust in Your plan, knowing that You are with me through every transition.

Change is not just something to fear; it's a canvas for your growth and discovery.

FINDING STRENGTH IN SCRIPTURE

"I can do all things through Christ who strengthens me."

Philippians 4:13

DEVOTION

In times of uncertainty, remember that the true strength you seek is not found in yourself, but in the unwavering promise of God's presence.

REFLECTION

What verses or stories in the Bible remind you that you are not alone in your struggles? How can you draw strength from these scriptures when anxiety feels overwhelming?

_____

_____

_____

_____

PRAYER

Dear Lord, thank You for always being our source of strength. Help me to remember Your words and find comfort in my moments of anxiety. I trust in Your promise to be with me always.

God's presence is a refuge; His words are a balm for the anxious heart.

THE GIFT
OF STILLNESS

"Be still before the Lord and wait patiently for Him; do not fret when people succeed in their ways, when they carry out their wicked schemes."

Psalm 37:7

DEVOTION

Take the time to sit quietly with your thoughts; sometimes, stillness reveals the answers your heart longs for.

REFLECTION

What does stillness look like in your life right now, and how might it open your heart to peace and clarity?

_____

_____

_____

_____

PRAYER

Dear God, thank you for the gift of quiet moments in our busy lives. Help me to seek and embrace stillness, finding comfort and strength in your presence.

Stillness is the gentle whisper of peace amid life's chaotic symphony.

HOPE FOR A NEW DAY

"But those who hope in the Lord will renew their strength. They will soar on wings like eagles; they will run and not grow weary, they will walk and not be faint."

Isaiah 40:31

DEVOTION

Hope is like the sunrise; no matter how dark the night, it brings the assurance that a new day awaits, ready to offer second chances and renewed strength.

REFLECTION

What does the idea of a new day mean for you when you feel weighed down by your worries? How can you embrace the freshness of hope as you step into today?

_____

_____

_____

_____

PRAYER

Dear God, thank You for the gift of a new day. Help me to see each morning as an opportunity for renewal and growth, filled with Your love and light.

Every dawn brings a chance to start again, casting aside yesterday's shadows.

BATTLING COMPARISON ON SOCIAL MEDIA

"Above all else, guard your heart, for everything you do flows from it"

Proverbs 4:23

DEVOTION

You are enough just as you are; your life story is beautifully unique and cannot be measured by the highlight reels of others.

REFLECTION

What do you feel when you scroll through social media and see what others are sharing? How often do you compare your life, look, or achievements to theirs?

_____

_____

_____

_____

PRAYER

Dear Lord, help me to find my worth in You and not in the images on my screen. Let me rest in the understanding that I am beautifully made, just as I am. Guide my heart to embrace my unique journey with confidence and grace.

Your value isn't measured by likes or followers; it's defined by the love that God has for you.

ACCEPTING
GOD'S GRACE

"From the fullness of his grace we have all received one blessing after another."

John 1:16

DEVOTION

Remember that grace is not a reward for perfection but a loving gift that frees us from the need to be anything other than who we truly are.

REFLECTION

What is one area in your life where you struggle to accept God's grace, and how might accepting that grace change your perspective today?

_____

_____

_____

_____

PRAYER

Dear Heavenly Father, thank you for the gift of grace that you freely give. Help me to open my heart and accept your love, reminding me that I am enough just as I am.

Grace is the gentle invitation to grow, not the burden of perfection.

FAITH OVER FEAR

"When I am afraid, I put my trust in you."

Psalm 56:3

DEVOTION

When fear arises, remember that your faith can be the anchor that steadies you through life's storms.

REFLECTION

What fears or worries do you find yourself facing most often? How might trusting in your faith change your perspective on those challenges?

_____

_____

_____

_____

PRAYER

Dear God, thank you for being our strength in moments of doubt. Help me to lean into my faith and let go of my fears, trusting that You are always with me.

Faith is the bridge that transforms fear into freedom.

INSPIRING AFFIRMATIONS FOR ANXIETY

"I sought the Lord, and he answered me; he delivered me from all my fears."

Psalm 34:4

DEVOTION

It's essential to remember that acknowledging your anxiety is the first step toward overcoming it, and you possess the strength to rise above your fears.

REFLECTION

What are some things that cause you to feel anxious, and how can you remind yourself of your strength in those moments?

_____

_____

_____

_____

PRAYER

Dear God, thank you for being our constant source of comfort. Help us lean on you when anxiety creeps in and remind us of the strength you've placed within us.

You are stronger than your fear, and each day is a chance to rise above it.

GOD LISTENS TO MY HEART

"O Lord, you have searched me and known me. You know when I sit down and when I rise up; you discern my thoughts from afar."

Psalm 139:1-2

DEVOTION

Life can be tumultuous, but in our vulnerability, we can find assurance that God truly hears our hearts and walks with us through every storm.

REFLECTION

What are the things that weigh heavily on your heart today, and how can you bring them to God in prayer? Consider the emotions that rise within you and invite God into those moments.

_____

_____

_____

_____

PRAYER

Dear God, thank You for always listening to my heart. Help me to remember that I can share my worries and dreams with You, knowing that You care deeply for me.

God hears the whispers of your heart long before you speak them aloud.

SELF-COMPASSION THROUGH CHRIST'S EYES

"Therefore, as God's chosen people, holy and dearly loved, clothe yourselves with compassion, kindness, humility, gentleness and patience. Bear with each other and forgive one another if any of you has a grievance against someone. Forgive as the Lord forgave you. And over all these virtues put on love, which binds them all together in perfect unity."

Colossians 3:12–14

DEVOTION

Embracing self–compassion is a journey of recognizing and forgiving our own shortcomings, just as we extend grace to others.

REFLECTION

What does it look like for you to show kindness to yourself when you're feeling anxious or overwhelmed? Can you name a few specific ways you can practice self-compassion today?

_____

_____

_____

_____

PRAYER

Dear Lord, help me to see myself through Your loving eyes. Remind me to extend grace and gentleness to my heart, just as You do. Amen.

Embracing your imperfections is the first step towards recognizing your worth in Christ.

IDENTITY
IN CHRIST

"I praise you because I am fearfully and wonderfully made; your works are wonderful, I know that full well."

Psalm 139:14

DEVOTION

The journey to understanding our true identity often begins with embracing the truth that we are wonderfully created by God, free from the burdens of comparison.

REFLECTION

What are some thoughts or feelings that you hold about yourself that might need to be rethought in light of who Christ says you are?

_____

_____

_____

_____

PRAYER

Dear God, thank You for loving me just as I am. Help me to see myself through Your eyes and to embrace my identity in You every day.

We find our true selves not in the world's standards, but in Christ's love and purpose for us.

DEALING WITH OVERWHELM

"When anxiety was great within me, your consolation brought me joy."

Psalm 94:19

DEVOTION

Finding moments to breathe and pause can remind us that we don't have to face our overwhelm alone; seeking comfort in faith can bring a profound sense of relief.

REFLECTION

What does feeling overwhelmed look like for you today, and how can you take a moment to step back and breathe?

_____

_____

_____

_____

PRAYER

Dear God, help me find peace in the midst of my chaos. Calm my racing thoughts and remind me that I am not alone in this struggle. Fill me with Your comfort and guidance.

The waves of overwhelm can seem towering, but remember, they cannot drown you; your foundation is built on solid ground.

BUILDING RESILIENCE

Proverbs 31:25 speaks of a woman "clothed with strength and dignity; she can laugh at the days to come."

DEVOTION

In life, resilience is found in turning our fears into opportunities for growth and connection.

REFLECTION

What moments in your life have challenged you the most, and how did you rise above those challenges?

_____

_____

_____

_____

PRAYER

Dear God, thank you for the strength you give us each day. Help me to embrace my challenges with courage and trust in your plan for my life. May I find joy in the journey as I grow stronger.

You have the power within you to turn every challenge into an opportunity for growth.

GOD'S TIMING IS PERFECT

"In their hearts humans plan their course, but the Lord establishes their steps."

Proverbs 16:9

DEVOTION

Sometimes, the waiting and the anxiety seem overwhelming; however, trusting in God's perfect timing can turn moments of doubt into opportunities for grace and growth.

REFLECTION

What area of your life feels uncertain right now, and how might trusting in God's timing change your perspective?

_____

_____

_____

_____

PRAYER

Dear God, help me to trust in Your perfect timing for my life. Grant me peace as I wait and the strength to lean on You, knowing You have a beautiful plan for me.

God's timing is like a beautifully woven tapestry; every thread matters in the grand design.

HEALTHY WAYS TO COPE WITH STRESS

"Anxiety weighs down the heart, but a kind word cheers it up."

Proverbs 12:25

DEVOTION

In times of stress, seeking solace in nature and taking moments for self-reflection can transform our anxiety into peace.

REFLECTION

What are some activities that bring you peace and joy when you feel overwhelmed by stress? How can you make time for these in your daily routine?

_____

_____

_____

_____

PRAYER

Dear God, thank you for being our steady anchor during tumultuous times. Help us to find joy in the little things and grant us the wisdom to know when to pause and breathe.

Finding calm in the chaos is a choice we can make every day.

LEARNING TO BREATHE DEEPLY

"Peace I leave with you; my peace I give you. I do not give to you as the world gives. Do not let your hearts be troubled and do not be afraid."

John 14:27

DEVOTION

In moments of anxiety, remember that taking a deep breath can be a sacred act of letting go—a reminder that, amidst life's challenges, you are held and loved.

REFLECTION

What does it feel like in your body when you take a deep breath? Can you slow down for a moment and notice the difference it makes?

_____

_____

_____

_____

PRAYER

Dear God, thank you for the gift of breathing and the peace it can bring. Help me find moments today to pause, inhale deeply, and release my worries into Your care.

In every breath, there lies a chance to release what weighs heavy and to invite calm within.

LETTİNG GO OF WHAT OTHERS THİNK

"Fear of man will prove to be a snare, but whoever trusts in the Lord is kept safe."

Proverbs 29:25

DEVOTION

Embracing who you are, apart from others' opinions, allows you to find peace and purpose in your own beautiful journey.

REFLECTION

What thoughts or fears hold you back from fully embracing who you are, free from the judgment of others?

_____

_____

_____

_____

PRAYER

Dear God, help me to embrace my true self and to release the weight of others' opinions. Fill my heart with courage as I learn to trust in Your love and purpose for my life.

Your worth is not determined by the whispers of others, but by the beautiful truth of who you are in Christ.

BELONGİNG İN GOD'S FAMILY

"Yet to all who did receive him, to those who believed in his name, he gave the right to become children of God."

John 1:12

DEVOTION

For every anxious heart, know that you are not alone; God's family wraps around you like a warm embrace, ready to welcome you home.

REFLECTION

What does it mean for you to feel like you truly belong, and how can you see yourself as a cherished member of God's family today?

_____

_____

_____

_____

PRAYER

Dear God, thank you for welcoming me into your family. Help me to feel your love and acceptance in my heart, reminding me that I always have a place with You.

In God's family, you are never alone; you are always held in His loving embrace.

RENEWING YOUR MIND

"Do not be conformed to this world, but be transformed by the renewal of your mind, that by testing you may discern what is the will of God, what is good and acceptable and perfect."

Romans 12:2

DEVOTION

Embrace the practice of renewing your thoughts, as it is a powerful tool for finding peace amid life's chaos.

REFLECTION

What thoughts weigh heavy on your heart today? Can you think of a time when you transformed a negative thought into something more hopeful? How did that change your perspective?

_____

_____

_____

_____

PRAYER

Dear God, please help me to guard my thoughts and focus on Your truth. Give me the strength to renew my mind each day and find peace in Your promises. Amen.

Your mind is a garden; you can choose what to plant and nurture.

CREATING A PEACEFUL SPACE

"For the mountains may depart and the hills be removed, but my steadfast love shall not depart from you, and my covenant of peace shall not be removed,"

Isaiah 54:10

DEVOTION

Sometimes, carving out a peaceful space in our lives is the first step in finding the calm we seek amidst the storm.

REFLECTION

What does your ideal peaceful space look like, and how can you recreate that calming feeling in your own life today?

_____

_____

_____

_____

PRAYER

Dear God, help me to create a peaceful space in my heart and mind. May I find comfort in Your presence and learn to embrace the quiet moments with You.

Peace is not the absence of chaos, but the presence of calm in your heart.

UNDERSTANDING YOUR TRIGGERS

"Search me, O God, and know my heart;
test me and know my anxious thoughts.
See if there is any offensive way in me,
and lead me in the way everlasting."

Psalm 139:23-24

DEVOTION

Understanding your triggers helps you
discern what truly stirs your heart,
allowing for healing and growth in the
presence of God's unwavering love.

REFLECTION

What are the situations or thoughts that make your heart race or your stomach twist, and how can you start to recognize these triggers in your daily life?

_____

_____

_____

_____

PRAYER

Dear God, please help me to understand my feelings and the triggers that affect me. Grant me the wisdom to navigate my emotions with grace and the strength to seek Your peace in anxious moments.

Understanding your triggers is the first step toward finding your calm.

GOD'S COMFORT IN SADNESS

"Wait for the Lord; be strong and take heart and wait for the Lord."

Psalm 27:14

DEVOTION

Even in the depths of sadness, embrace the creative process God offers, knowing that beauty can arise from your heartache.

REFLECTION

What sadness have you been carrying in your heart lately? How can you invite God into that space to bring you comfort and peace?

_____

_____

_____

_____

PRAYER

Dear God, thank You for being my safe place when I'm feeling down. Help me to feel Your love and presence wrap around me, reminding me that I'm never alone in my sadness.

In every tear we shed, God collects and cherishes our pain, turning it into paths of comfort and strength.

TURNİNG WORRY INTO WORSHİP

"Cast your burdens on the Lord, and He will sustain you; He will never permit the righteous to be moved."

Psalm 55:22

DEVOTION

The journey from worry to worship can transform our anxious hearts into vessels of peace, reminding us that God is always in control.

REFLECTION

What worry are you holding onto right now that may be keeping you from feeling God's peace? How would your life change if you surrendered that worry to Him?

_____

_____

_____

_____

PRAYER

Dear God, thank You for being my comfort and strength. Help me to turn my worries into moments of worship, trusting in Your love and guidance.

When we release our worries to God, we open ourselves to His peace.

MANAGING FOMO (FEAR OF MISSING OUT)

"Rejoice always, pray continually, give thanks in all circumstances; for this is God's will for you in Christ Jesus."

1 Thessalonians 5:16–18

DEVOTION

In cultivating gratitude for our own lives and experiences, we help soothe the anxious heart and shift the focus from what we lack to the abundance that surrounds us.

REFLECTION

What events or gatherings make you feel like you're missing out? Have there been moments when the pressure to join in took away from what truly makes you happy and fulfilled?

_____

_____

_____

_____

PRAYER

Dear God, help me find peace in the moments I struggle with feeling left out. Remind me that my worth is not defined by social events but by Your love and purpose for my life. Fill my heart with contentment and joy.

Sometimes, being still means you're right where you need to be.

ASKİNG
FOR HELP

"The name of the Lord is a fortified tower; the righteous run to it and are safe."

Proverbs 18:10

DEVOTION

Remember, it's not a sign of weakness, but a courageous step towards growth when you reach out for help and let others in.

REFLECTION

What does asking for help mean to you, and how do you feel when you think about reaching out to someone for support? Are there fears or misconceptions that hold you back?

_____

_____

_____

_____

PRAYER

Dear God, thank you for being our refuge and strength. Help me to remember that it's okay to ask for help and that I am never alone in my struggles. Amen.

Reaching out is not a sign of weakness; it's a step towards strength.

SILENCING NEGATIVE SELF-TALK

"We demolish arguments and every pretension that sets itself up against the knowledge of God, and we take captive every thought to make it obedient to Christ."

2 Corinthians 10:5

DEVOTION

Every negative thought is not a fact; it can simply be a feeling that needs to be challenged and redirected.

REFLECTION

What negative thoughts do you find yourself repeating about yourself? How do they affect the way you see yourself and the world around you?

_____

_____

_____

_____

PRAYER

Dear God, help me to recognize and silence the negative words that fill my mind. Teach me to embrace Your truth about who I am and to find peace in Your love. Amen.

Your voice matters; choose to let it be kind and uplifting.

FAITH-FILLED JOURNALING

"But the fruit of the Spirit is love, joy, peace, forbearance, kindness, goodness, faithfulness, gentleness, and self-control."

Galatians 5:22-23

DEVOTION

In the simple act of journaling, we can reveal the inner workings of our hearts and experience God's peace flowing through the ink.

REFLECTION

What words do you think God is waiting to hear from you? How can journaling help you share your worries, joys, and dreams with Him?

_____

_____

_____

_____

PRAYER

Dear God, thank You for being a safe space where I can pour out my heart. Help me find the courage to write down my feelings and trust that You are with me every step of the way.

Your journal is a sacred place where your soul can bloom, even in the midst of anxiety.

CALMING NIGHTTIME ANXIETIES

"When you lie down, you will not be afraid; when you lie down, your sleep will be sweet."

Proverbs 3:24

DEVOTION

Sometimes all we need is a safe space to express our worries and fears, allowing us to find calm amidst the chaos.

REFLECTION

What thoughts flood your mind as you lay down at night? How can you release those anxieties and find peace in the quiet moments?

_____

_____

_____

_____

PRAYER

Dear God, as night falls and worries creep in, help me find comfort in Your presence. Let Your peace wash over my heart and guide my thoughts so I can rest in Your love.

Peace is not the absence of anxiety; it is the presence of a greater love.

LOVE THAT NEVER LEAVES

"For God so loved the world that He gave His one and only Son."

John 3:16

DEVOTION

Love is a constant, unwavering presence that meets us in our vulnerability and helps us rise above our fears.

REFLECTION

What does it feel like to know that there is a love surrounding you, no matter the challenges you face? How might it change your perspective if you truly believed that love is always there for you?

_____

_____

_____

_____

PRAYER

Dear God, thank you for your unwavering love that surrounds me every day. Help me to feel comforted by your presence, especially during anxious moments. Guide me to trust in this love and let it bring me peace.

Your worth is not defined by the storms you weather, but by the love that never leaves.

FACİNG FEARS WİTH PRAYER

"Look at the birds of the air; they do not sow or reap or store away in barns, and yet your heavenly Father feeds them. Are you not much more valuable than they?"

Matthew 6:26

DEVOTION

When anxiety creeps in, turning to prayer can illuminate the path to courage and reassurance.

REFLECTION

What fears are you facing today that feel too big to handle on your own? How can you invite God into those moments to help you find peace?

_____

_____

_____

_____

PRAYER

Dear God, help me to surrender my fears to You. Give me courage as I face the things that scare me, and remind me that I am never alone when I walk with You.

Prayer is the bridge that leads us from fear to faith.

TURNİNG MİSTAKES İNTO LESSONS

"Consider it pure joy, my sisters, whenever you face trials of many kinds, because you know that the testing of your faith produces perseverance."

James 1:2-3

DEVOTION

Mistakes are not failures; they are valuable lessons that guide us toward our true potential.

REFLECTION

What mistakes have you made recently that made you feel anxious or worried? How can you reflect on these experiences to find the lessons hidden within them?

_____

_____

_____

_____

PRAYER

Dear God, thank you for walking with me through my struggles. Help me to see that my mistakes are opportunities for growth and to trust in Your plan for my life. Amen.

Every stumble on the path is just a step toward wisdom.

EMBRACING IMPERFECTION

"Come to me, all you who are weary and burdened, and I will give you rest. Take my yoke upon you and learn from me, for I am gentle and humble in heart, and you will find rest for your souls. For my yoke is easy and my burden is light."

Matthew 11:28–30

DEVOTION

Embracing our imperfections can lead to discovering the beauty and joy within ourselves that we never realized was there.

REFLECTION

What parts of yourself do you struggle to accept, and how might embracing your imperfections help you grow?

_____

_____

_____

_____

PRAYER

Dear God, thank you for creating me just as I am. Help me to see my imperfections as beautiful and unique markers of my journey, and remind me that I am perfectly made in your eyes.

Embracing imperfections reveals the beauty of our journey.

THE BLESSING OF TRUE FRIENDS

"The heartfelt counsel of a friend is as sweet as perfume and incense."

Proverbs 27:9

DEVOTION

True friends not only lift our spirits but also remind us that we're never alone in our struggles.

REFLECTION

What does it mean to you to have true friends in your life, and how can you appreciate them more this week?

_____

_____

_____

_____

PRAYER

Dear Lord, thank you for the gift of friendship. Help me to nurture the true friends in my life and to be a blessing to them as they are to me. Amen.

True friends see you as you are, but they also help you grow into who you're meant to be.

GUARDING YOUR HEART AND MIND

"For everything there is a season, and a time for every matter under heaven."

Ecclesiastes 3:1

DEVOTION

Life may seem daunting, but by creating a safe space for ourselves and our feelings, we invite peace into our lives, gently guarding our hearts and minds against anxiety.

REFLECTION

What thoughts or feelings are currently weighing heavy on your heart, and how can you invite God into those areas to help you find peace and clarity?

_____

_____

_____

_____

PRAYER

Dear God, help me to guard my heart and mind from negativity and anxiety. Fill me with your peace and remind me of your love in every moment of uncertainty.

Your heart is a garden; protect it from weeds that choke the flowers of joy.

RELEASING CONTROL

"Consider it pure joy, my brothers and sisters,[a] whenever you face trials of many kinds, because you know that the testing of your faith produces perseverance. Let perseverance finish its work so that you may be mature and complete, not lacking anything."

James 1:2–4

DEVOTION

Sometimes, letting go of control is the first step toward experiencing the peace that comes from embracing life's uncertainties.

REFLECTION

What is one area of your life where you feel the need to control the outcome, and how might releasing that control bring you peace?

_____

_____

_____

_____

PRAYER

Dear God, help me let go of my worries and trust in Your plan for my life. Remind me that I am not alone and that Your presence brings comfort in every situation. Amen.

Releasing control opens the door to new possibilities and freedoms, inviting peace into our hearts.

GOD'S CARE IN SMALL DETAILS

"The steadfast love of the Lord never ceases; His mercies never come to an end; they are new every morning; great is your faithfulness."

Lamentations 3:22–23

DEVOTION

Every detail of our lives is known by God; we can find peace in the assurance that He actively cares for us, soothing our anxieties with unexpected reminders of His presence.

REFLECTION

What are some small details in your life that you think God cares about? How might seeing those moments as part of His love change your perspective?

_____

_____

_____

_____

PRAYER

Dear God, thank you for being present in every part of my life. Help me to notice and appreciate the small ways You show Your love each day. Amen.

God's care wraps around us in the little things, reminding us we're never alone.

DEALING WITH FAMILY STRESS

"And we know that in all things God works for the good of those who love him, who have been called according to his purpose."

Romans 8:28

DEVOTION

When facing family stress, remember that God is weaving every situation into His perfect plan, and love can still shine through the challenges.

REFLECTION

What pressures do you feel from your family, and how can you bring those concerns to God for comfort and understanding?

_____

_____

_____

_____

PRAYER

Dear God, help me to navigate the stress within my family with grace and patience. Grant me the strength to communicate openly and the wisdom to understand their perspectives.

Sometimes, the strongest bridges are built through understanding and love.

CHOOSING JOY

"Weeping may last for the night, but joy comes in the morning."

Psalm 30:5

DEVOTION

Choose to seek joy in every circumstance, knowing that sometimes it's a decision we make each day, just like the sun rises again after the night.

REFLECTION

What brings you joy, even on your hardest days? How can you choose to focus on those moments amidst your worries?

_____

_____

_____

_____

PRAYER

Dear God, thank You for the gift of joy that You offer, even in our anxious times. Help me to open my heart and discover the moments that bring a smile to my face today.

Joy is not the absence of troubles, but the presence of hope and laughter in the midst of them.

ENCOURAGING OTHERS

"Therefore encourage one another and build each other up, just as in fact you are doing."

1 Thessalonians 5:11

DEVOTION

In the tapestry of our lives, the threads of encouragement we weave for one another create a beautiful fabric of resilience and hope.

REFLECTION

What does encouraging someone else look like in your daily life, and how can you take small steps today to uplift those around you?

_____

_____

_____

_____

PRAYER

Dear God, help me to see the beauty in others and inspire me to share kind words and support. May my heart be open to encourage those who need it most.

Your words have the power to lighten someone's day and lift their spirit.

PRAYING FOR PEACE

"You will keep in perfect peace those whose minds are steadfast, because they trust in you."

Isaiah 26:3

DEVOTION

Trusting in God's presence can transform those anxious moments into opportunities for connection and growth.

REFLECTION

What are the storms in your life that feel overwhelming, and how might inviting peace into your heart change your perspective?

_____

_____

_____

_____

PRAYER

Dear God, please wrap me in your calming presence today. Help me to let go of my worries and embrace the tranquility that comes from trusting You. Amen.

Peace is not found in the absence of turmoil, but in the presence of God.

FINDING CONTENTMENT

"Delight yourself in the Lord, and He will give you the desires of your heart."

Psalm 37:4

DEVOTION

True contentment comes from appreciating the gifts in your life and finding joy in the present moment rather than chasing after what others have or what you think you lack.

REFLECTION

What does contentment look like in your life right now? Can you think of a specific moment when you felt truly at peace, free from worries or comparisons?

_____

_____

_____

_____

PRAYER

Dear God, help me to find my peace in You. Teach me to embrace the gifts in my life with gratitude and joy. Fill my heart with a spirit of contentment today.

Contentment blooms when we choose to see the beauty in our own journey.

LETTİNG GO
OF PAST MİSTAKES

"For I will forgive their wickedness and will remember their sins no more."

Hebrews 8:12

DEVOTION

Letting go of past mistakes allows us to embrace the beautiful journey of growth and healing, reminding us that we are continually being made new.

REFLECTION

What past mistakes are you holding onto that keep you from moving forward? How might letting go of these burdens transform your path ahead?

_____

_____

_____

_____

PRAYER

Dear God, help me to release the weight of my past mistakes. Fill my heart with Your love and grace, reminding me that I am always this moment's reflection, not just my past choices.

Your past does not define you; it merely prepares you for the beautiful journey ahead.

TRUSTING GOD'S PLAN

"Now faith is confidence in what we hope for and assurance about what we do not see."

Hebrews 11:1

DEVOTION

Trusting in God's plan means embracing the journey, allowing yourself the grace to grow amidst the uncertainties, and knowing that every step taken is part of a larger, beautiful design woven specifically for you.

REFLECTION

What worries do you carry in your heart today, and how might letting go of those burdens help you to trust more deeply in God's plan for your life?

_____

_____

_____

_____

PRAYER

Dear God, thank You for always being with me, even in the midst of my worries. Please help me to trust in Your plan for my life and give me the strength to rise above my anxieties.

Trusting God's plan means believing that He can write a story more beautiful than we could ever imagine.

FAİTH WHEN YOU FEEL INVİSİBLE

"Are not five sparrows sold for two pennies? And yet not one of them is forgotten by God. Indeed, the very hairs of your head are all numbered. Don't be afraid; you are worth more than many sparrows."

Luke 12:6-7

DEVOTION

When you feel invisible, remember that your worth is far greater than the moments of isolation; God sees you and cherishes you just as you are.

REFLECTION

What moments have made you feel invisible recently, and how might God's presence help you see your worth in those times?

_____

_____

_____

_____

PRAYER

Dear God, please remind me that I am seen and loved, even on the days when I feel invisible. Help me to find peace in your presence and know that I am never alone.

In moments of feeling unseen, remember that your true worth is found in the eyes of the One who created you.

CALM IN SOCIAL SITUATIONS

"Never will I leave you; never will I forsake you."

Hebrews 13:5

DEVOTION

Embrace the truth that you are never alone in your social interactions; draw from the support and acceptance of those around you.

REFLECTION

What thoughts run through your mind when you find yourself in a crowded room or a social gathering? How do you feel in those moments, and how might you invite peace into your heart instead of anxiety?

_____

_____

_____

_____

PRAYER

Dear God, when I feel anxious in social situations, please remind me of Your presence. Help me to breathe deeply and trust that I am never alone, for Your love surrounds me always.

Peace isn't found in the absence of chaos, but in the presence of calm within.

GOD'S STRENGTH
IN MY WEAKNESS

"But he said to me, 'My grace is sufficient for you, for my power is made perfect in weakness.' Therefore, I will boast all the more gladly about my weaknesses, so that Christ's power may rest on me."

2 Corinthians 12:9

DEVOTION

Our greatest moments of resilience often emerge from acknowledging our weaknesses and allowing God's grace to carry us through.

REFLECTION

What are some areas in your life where you feel weak or anxious, and how could you invite God into those moments to find strength?

_____

_____

_____

_____

PRAYER

Dear God, thank you for being my refuge in times of weakness. Help me to lean on you when I feel overwhelmed, trusting that your strength will carry me through.

In my weakness, I discover the depth of Your strength.

LEARNING TO FORGIVE YOURSELF

"I, even I, am he who blots out your transgressions, for my own sake, and remembers your sins no more."

Isaiah 43:25

DEVOTION

Forgiving ourselves is not a sign of weakness but rather a profound act of strength and grace that enables us to grow and flourish.

REFLECTION

What are the moments in your life where you find it hardest to forgive yourself? Think about how you can begin to take steps towards healing those feelings and letting go of the past.

_____

_____

_____

_____

PRAYER

Dear God, help me to embrace your grace and learn to forgive myself just as you have forgiven me. Let your love remind me that I am worthy of peace and healing.

Forgiveness begins within; it's the gentle act of releasing the weight we carry.

HOPE FOR A BETTER TOMORROW

"There is surely a future hope for you,
and your hope will not be cut off."

Proverbs 23:18

DEVOTION

Even in the midst of anxiety, believing in
a brighter future can transform your
outlook and lead to healing connections.

REFLECTION

What dreams or hopes do you hold in your heart for tomorrow, and how can you take small steps to nurture them today?

_____

_____

_____

_____

PRAYER

Dear God, thank You for the hope that illuminates even the darkest days. Help me to trust in Your plan for my life and fill me with peace as I look toward the future.

Even the smallest flicker of hope can light the way through the darkest nights.

BUILDING A SUPPORT SYSTEM

"Be completely humble and gentle; be patient, bearing with one another in love. Make every effort to keep the unity of the Spirit through the bond of peace."

Ephesians 4:2-3

DEVOTION

True strength lies in the connections we foster with those around us, reminding us that we are never truly alone in our struggles.

REFLECTION

What does your ideal support system look like, and who do you feel safe sharing your thoughts and feelings with?

_____

_____

_____

_____

PRAYER

Dear God, please guide me in building meaningful connections with those around me. Help me to open my heart and surround myself with people who uplift and encourage me.

True strength lies in the relationships we cultivate and the love we share.

EMBRACING QUIET MOMENTS

"In repentance and rest is your salvation, in quietness and trust is your strength."

Isaiah 30:15

DEVOTION

Sometimes, the quiet moments we carve out for ourselves hold the most profound strength and clarity.

REFLECTION

What does it feel like in your heart
when you find a quiet moment to
yourself? Can you recall a time when
stillness brought you peace?

_____

_____

_____

_____

PRAYER

Dear God, help me to cherish the quiet
moments in my life. May I find comfort
and strength in your presence, even
amidst the noise around me. Amen.

*In the stillness, we find the
whispers of our hearts and the
voice of God.*

SEEING YOURSELF AS GOD SEES YOU

"But the Lord said to Samuel, 'Do not consider his appearance or his height, for I have rejected him. The Lord does not look at the things people look at. People look at the outward appearance, but the Lord looks at the heart.'"

1 Samuel 16:7

DEVOTION

We are often our harshest critics, but God invites us to see our beauty through His eyes and to embrace our unique inner light.

REFLECTION

What would it feel like to look in the mirror and see the beauty that God sees in you? What labels or doubts are you carrying that don't match His view of you?

_____

_____

_____

_____

PRAYER

Dear God, help me to see myself through Your loving eyes. Remind me every day of my worth and the beauty that You've placed within me. May I embrace the unique girl You created me to be.

You are a masterpiece, crafted with purpose and designed for greatness.

RELEASING WHAT YOU CAN'T CONTROL

"Never will I leave you; never will I forsake you." So we say with confidence, "The Lord is my helper; I will not be afraid."

Hebrews 13:5b-6

DEVOTION

Life often teaches us that releasing control can lead to unexpected joys and bonds.

REFLECTION

What is one thing in your life right now that you wish you could control, but deep down you know it's beyond your reach? How does holding onto that feeling affect your peace and joy?

_____

_____

_____

_____

PRAYER

Dear God, as I navigate this journey, help me to release my grip on the things I cannot control. Fill my heart with Your peace, guiding me to trust in Your plans for me.

Freedom comes when we let go of the weight that is not ours to carry.

PRACTICING MINDFULNESS WITH GOD

"Be still before the Lord and wait patiently for Him."

Psalm 37:7a

DEVOTION

In the midst of life's chaos, taking a moment to be still with God can transform anxiety into peace.

REFLECTION

What moments throughout your day make you feel most anxious, and how might you invite God into those moments to find peace?

_____

_____

_____

_____

PRAYER

Dear God, help me to slow down and breathe, to find Your presence in the chaos of my thoughts. Thank You for being my anchor in the storm, guiding me to a place of stillness.

Finding stillness in the storm is where you'll meet God most intimately.

UNPLUGGING FROM TECHNOLOGY

"Therefore, since we are surrounded by such a great cloud of witnesses, let us throw off everything that hinders and the sin that so easily entangles. And let us run with perseverance the race marked out for us, 2 fixing our eyes on Jesus, the pioneer and perfecter of faith. For the joy set before him he endured the cross, scorning its shame, and sat down at the right hand of the throne of God."

Hebrews 12:1-2

DEVOTION

In a world where technology often overshadows our inner thoughts, take the time to step back and discover the beauty and clarity that comes from unplugging.

REFLECTION

What does it feel like for you to take a break from your phone or social media? Can you recall a time when disconnecting brought you peace or clarity?

_____

_____

_____

_____

PRAYER

Dear God, help me to find moments today when I can unplug and reconnect with Your presence. Give me the strength to step away from technology and embrace the beauty in stillness.

Sometimes the quietest moments speak the loudest to our hearts.

TURNING ANXIOUS ENERGY INTO ACTION

"Commit your way to the Lord; trust in Him and He will act."

Psalm 37:5

DEVOTION

When faced with anxiety, remember that even small, purposeful actions can lead you to a place of peace and clarity.

REFLECTION

What anxious thoughts are swirling in your mind right now, and how might you turn that energy into meaningful action today?

_____

_____

_____

_____

PRAYER

Dear God, please help me transform my worry into strength and courage. Guide me to take small steps forward, knowing that You are with me every moment.

Anxiety can be the spark that ignites your passion when you let it propel you forward.

FAİTH DURİNG DİSAPPOİNTMENT

"Not only so, but we also glory in our sufferings, because we know that suffering produces perseverance; 4 perseverance, character; and character, hope. 5 And hope does not put us to shame, because God's love has been poured out into our hearts through the Holy Spirit, who has been given to us."

Romans 5:3-5

DEVOTION

What may feel like a setback today can be a stepping stone toward something more significant in God's unfolding plan.

REFLECTION

What disappointments are you currently facing, and how might your faith guide you through these challenging moments?

_____

_____

_____

_____

PRAYER

Dear God, help me to trust in Your plan even when things don't go my way. Remind me that You are with me in my struggles, and that Your love never wavers.

Faith is the bridge that carries us over the chasms of our disappointments.

TRUSTING GOD IN FRIENDSHIPS

"I no longer call you servants, because a servant does not know his master's business. Instead, I have called you friends, for everything that I learned from my Father I have made known to you."

John 15:15

DEVOTION

Sometimes, placing our trust in God opens doors to friendships that nurture rather than drain us.

REFLECTION

What does it mean for you to trust God in your friendships? How might leaning on Him change the way you relate to your friends or handle conflicts?

_____

_____

_____

_____

PRAYER

Dear God, thank You for the gift of friendship. Help me to lean on You as I navigate my relationships, knowing that You guide and support me in every interaction.

Trusting God opens the door to the most beautiful friendships.

COPING WITH PEER PRESSURE

Psalm 121:1-2 reminds us, "I lift my eyes to the hills—where does my help come from? My help comes from the Lord, the Maker of heaven and earth."

DEVOTION

Be assured that standing firm in your choices not only honors your values but often inspires others to do the same.

REFLECTION

What situations make you feel the strongest pull to conform to what your friends are doing? How can you stay true to yourself in those moments?

_____

_____

_____

_____

PRAYER

Dear God, thank You for always being with us through our challenges. Help us to find courage in You when we face peer pressure and to remember our true worth.

Staying true to yourself is the most beautiful gift you can give to the world.

RELEASING FEAR OF FAILURE

"So do not throw away your confidence; it will be richly rewarded. You need to persevere so that when you have done the will of God, you will receive what he has promised."

Hebrews 10:35-36

DEVOTION

Remember, dear one, that fear of failure can often hold you back from experiencing the beautiful plans God has for you.

REFLECTION

What are some fears about failure that keep you from pursuing your dreams, and how might you reframe those fears into stepping stones for growth?

_____

_____

_____

_____

PRAYER

Dear God, I come to You with my worries about failure. Help me to trust in Your plan for my life and to understand that every setback can lead to a new beginning. Grant me the courage to embrace my journey without fear.

Failure is not the end; it is a stepping stone to success.

FINDING
REST IN GOD

"There remains, then, a Sabbath-rest for the people of God; for anyone who enters God's rest also rests from their works, just as God did from his. Let us, therefore, make every effort to enter that rest, so that no one will perish by following their example of disobedience."

Hebrews 4:9–11

DEVOTION

Remember to carve out moments in your life for stillness and reflection, for it is in those spaces that God's peace can envelop you.

REFLECTION

What do you think it feels like to truly rest in God, and how can you take a moment today to invite Him into your worries?

_____

_____

_____

_____

PRAYER

Dear God, thank You for being a sanctuary in my chaos. Help me to find peace in Your presence, releasing my anxieties into Your caring hands.

Rest isn't just a break from our worries; it's a trust fall into the arms of God.

LEARNING TO CELEBRATE SMALL WINS

"Brothers and sisters, I do not consider myself yet to have taken hold of it. But one thing I do: Forgetting what is behind and straining toward what is ahead, I press on toward the goal to win the prize for which God has called me heavenward in Christ Jesus."

Philippians 3:13-14

DEVOTION

Every tiny step forward deserves recognition; celebrating small wins nurtures gratitude and encourages growth in our lives, no matter how insignificant they may seem.

REFLECTION

What are some small wins you've experienced this week, and how did they make you feel?

_____

_____

_____

_____

PRAYER

Dear Lord, thank You for the little moments of joy that fill our days. Help me to see and celebrate the small wins in my life, recognizing Your presence in each one.

Even the smallest victory holds the spark of hope and joy.

LISTENING FOR GOD'S VOICE

"My sheep hear my voice, and I know them, and they follow me."

John 10:27

DEVOTION

When we silence the noise around us, we open our hearts to truly hear God's gentle guidance and reassurance.

REFLECTION

What does it feel like to truly quiet your mind and listen for God's voice amidst your worries and uncertainties? Can you recall a moment when you felt a gentle nudge, as if God was communicating with you personally?

_____

_____

_____

_____

PRAYER

Dear God, help me to find stillness in my heart and open my ears to hear Your voice. Guide me through my anxiety and let your words of peace surround me. Thank you for being my constant companion.

Listening for God's voice is a journey, not a race; it's in the stillness where we often find clarity.

GOD'S LOVE
NEVER QUITS

"Give thanks to the Lord, for He is good.
His love endures forever."

Psalm 136:1

DEVOTION

God's love is a constant assurance that
helps us bloom, even in the most
anxious seasons of our lives.

REFLECTION

What's one area in your life where you feel like giving up, and how could you invite God into that situation? What might change if you remember His never-quit love for you?

_____

_____

_____

PRAYER

Dear God, thank You for loving me unconditionally, even when I feel overwhelmed. Help me to feel Your presence in my life and to trust that Your love will not fail.

God's love is a constant anchor in the stormy seas of life.

BEING HONEST ABOUT YOUR STRUGGLES

"Therefore confess your sins to each other and pray for each other so that you may be healed."

James 5:16

DEVOTION

Honesty about our struggles can forge deeper connections and pave the way for healing in ourselves and others.

REFLECTION

What is one struggle you're facing right now that feels too heavy to share with someone else? How might speaking about it lighten your heart?

_____

_____

_____

_____

PRAYER

Dear God, help me to be brave enough to share my struggles with others. May I find comfort in knowing I am not alone, and may Your love surround me as I seek to be honest with myself and those around me.

Honesty about your struggles is the first step to true healing.

AFFIRMING YOUR WORTH

"You are precious in my sight, and honored, and I love you."

Isaiah 43:4a

DEVOTION

Your true worth isn't determined by external validation but rather by the unique beauty God has placed within you.

REFLECTION

What does it mean to you to truly believe in your worth, especially when you face challenges or compare yourself to others? How can you remind yourself of your unique value each day?

_____

_____

_____

_____

PRAYER

Dear God, help me to see the beauty in who I am and embrace my worth. May I feel your love surrounding me, guiding me to recognize my strengths and the light within me.

You are precious, just as you are, and your worth is not defined by the opinions of others.

GIVING YOUR WORRIES TO GOD

"But even if you should suffer for what is right, you are blessed. Do not fear their threats; do not be frightened."

1 Peter 3:14

DEVOTION

Life can be daunting, but finding a quiet moment to share your worries with God can bring the peace you crave amidst the chaos.

REFLECTION

What worries are you holding onto right now that you could take a moment to give to God? How might your day change if you surrendered those burdens?

_____

_____

_____

_____

PRAYER

Dear God, help me to let go of my worries and trust in Your plan for my life. Please remind me that I am never alone, and that You are always there to guide and comfort me. Amen.

Your worries are not too heavy for His hands.

FINDING PURPOSE IN PAIN

"The Lord watches over those who fear him, those who rely on his unfailing love."

Psalm 33:18

DEVOTION

Emotional struggles can become the catalyst for discovering hidden talents and passions, transforming our pain into purpose that illuminates not just our lives but also the lives of those around us.

REFLECTION

What is one way your pain has shaped your perspective on life or your dreams for the future?

_____

_____

_____

_____

PRAYER

Dear God, help me to see the purpose in my pain. Give me the strength to trust in Your plan and the wisdom to grow from my experiences. Amen.

Even in the darkest moments, our struggles can illuminate the path to our purpose.

SETTING BOUNDARIES WITH LOVE

"Whether you turn to the right or to the left, your ears will hear a voice behind you saying, 'This is the way; walk in it."

Isaiah 30:21

DEVOTION

The lesson we can learn from Lily's story is that establishing boundaries is not an act of selfishness but a necessary aspect of self-care that allows us to nurture the relationships that matter most.

REFLECTION

What are some areas in your life where you feel you need to set boundaries, and how could doing so lead to a healthier, more fulfilling connection with those around you?

_____

_____

_____

_____

PRAYER

Dear God, help me to find the strength and wisdom to set boundaries that reflect love and care for myself and others. May I feel Your guidance in every conversation and recognize my worth as I navigate these important choices.

Setting boundaries is a way of loving yourself and inviting others to respect your heart.

SEEING GOD IN EVERYDAY MOMENTS

"Who of you by worrying can add a single hour to your life? Since you cannot do this very little thing, why do you worry about the rest?"

Luke 12:25-26

DEVOTION

In every ordinary day, there's an extraordinary presence of peace waiting for us to recognize it.

REFLECTION

What are some small moments today where you noticed God's presence or felt His love, even in the midst of your worries?

_____

_____

_____

_____

PRAYER

Dear God, help me to open my eyes to see You in the little things today. Thank You for being with me in both the joyful moments and the challenging ones.

Even in the chaos of life, God is whispering His love through the smallest details.

CELEBRATING YOUR UNIQUENESS

"For we are God's masterpiece. He has created us anew in Christ Jesus, so we can do the good things he planned for us long ago."

Ephesians 2:10

DEVOTION

Embracing one's uniqueness can lead to unexpected joy and connection, reminding us that we are all masterpieces crafted by the Divine.

REFLECTION

What makes you feel most like yourself?
When do you feel your unique gifts
shine the brightest? Take a moment to
think about the moments when you're
truly you—what do you love?

_____

_____

_____

_____

PRAYER

Dear God, thank you for creating me
uniquely and fearfully. Help me to
embrace who I am, celebrating my gifts
and quirks as I learn to shine in my own
special way. Amen.

*Your uniqueness is a beautiful
gift that the world needs.*

EMBRACING
NEW BEGINNINGS

"See, I am doing a new thing! Now it springs up; do you not perceive it? I am making a way in the wilderness and streams in the wasteland."

Isaiah 43:19

DEVOTION

Don't let fear hold you back; new beginnings often lead to the most beautiful parts of life.

REFLECTION

What new beginnings are you feeling anxious about right now, and how can you take a moment to breathe and reflect on the possibilities they might bring?

_____

_____

_____

_____

PRAYER

Dear God, thank you for the gift of new beginnings. Help this young heart to embrace the changes ahead with hope and courage, trusting in Your loving guidance.

Every ending is a new beginning waiting to unfold.

PEACE THAT PASSES UNDERSTANDING

"And the peace of God, which transcends all understanding, will guard your hearts and your minds in Christ Jesus."

Philippians 4:7

DEVOTION

In life, it's essential to pause, allowing God's peace to guard our hearts amidst the noise of our worries.

REFLECTION

What worries are filling your mind today, and how might you invite God's peace into those moments of anxiety? Consider how surrendering your fears to Him can bring a calm that surpasses what you can understand.

_____

_____

_____

_____

PRAYER

Dear God, thank you for being with me in my anxious moments. Help me to trust in Your peace that fills my heart and mind, guiding me through the storm. Amen.

His peace is like a gentle breeze that whispers hope into the chaos of your heart.

REMEMBERING GOD'S FAITHFULNESS

"Know therefore that the Lord your God is God; he is the faithful God, keeping his covenant of love to a thousand generations of those who love him and keep his commands."

Deuteronomy 7:9

DEVOTION

When our world feels like a storm, God's faithfulness is the anchor that steadies our hearts.

REFLECTION

What are some moments in your life when you've seen God's faithfulness, even in your anxious times?

_____

_____

_____

_____

PRAYER

Dear God, thank you for always being there for me, even when I feel overwhelmed. Help me to trust in Your faithfulness and remember that I am never alone.

God's faithfulness shines the brightest in our darkest moments.

HOW HAS THIS DEVOTIONAL HELPED YOU?

Hi there,

If these daily readings have given you comfort, clarity, or a sense of peace during overwhelming moments, I'd love to hear your story. Your experience may encourage another teen girl who feels anxious or unsure of where to turn.

To share your review, just scan the QR code below or type the link into your browser. Your words can offer hope to someone who needs it.

https://go.binnovatedigital.com/teengirlsanx

www.ingramcontent.com/pod-product-compliance
Lightning Source LLC
Chambersburg PA
CBHW071743120626
46550CB00002B/642